3:00 A.M.
Meditations for the
Middle of the Night

Dedicated to the
First Christian Church
Concord, California
on the occasion of its
100th Anniversary
May 5, 1985

RICHARD A. WING

3:00 A.M.
Meditations for the
Middle of the Night

ARTHUR PUBLISHING
P. O. Box 33213
San Diego, California 92103-0400

Cover design by Mara Hawkins
(based on René Magritte's painting, *The Enchanted Domain*)

*Special thanks to Industrial Graphic Arts, Concord, California: Lisle
and Ruth Morseman, John Morseman, Beth Shelton, and Ed Nyberg*

ISBN 0-934849-00-5

Grateful thanks to my wife
Shirley
for her skills in criticism
and typesetting

Special thanks to
Bill and Bev Plambeck
who made this book possible

Introduction

F. Scott Fitzgerald wrote: "in the deep dark recesses of the soul it is always 3 A.M." Some would call that existential time, the moment when you are truly alone, except for your own thoughts. It matters not in that hour if there is someone next to you. In that waking moment you are more alone than you might think; your *true* thoughts your only company. And in those moments you discover the difference between what you *say* you believe, and what you *really* believe. Courage is rare at that hour, and for some, courage is found in that hour.

These meditations are a collection of stories, quotes and personal thoughts that were true for me at 3:00 A.M. When first read, these stories seemed to leap off the page into an empty place in me. Sometimes I was aware of that empty spot. Sometimes I didn't know the empty place existed, until I read a better story than my own. With the hope that you might find among these a better story than the one you live right now, I write.

These meditations are dedicated to the First Christian Church of Concord, California, as the congregation celebrates its 100th Anniversary of caring and sharing.

One Shaft of Grace

Dr. Richard Selzer gave a sermon at the dedication of the Hope Unitarian Church in Tulsa, Oklahoma, October, 1977. As a Jewish boy growing up in a very Catholic neighborhood in Troy, New York, he somehow found himself attending a Mass. Upon leaving the sanctuary, he noted a dead fly floating on the Holy water. He plucked it out, only to be pounced upon by a priest who accused him of taking a penny from the side of the fount. He is duly accused of something he did not do and leaves the sanctuary never to enter again. This medical doctor now stands before a Unitarian Church as they dedicate their sanctuary. He tells the story at the Holy water fount, and then concludes by saying:

"**F**orgive me. I suppose that it (this story) has festered too long in my bosom. At last the world shall know why I never go to church.

"In spite of it all, I believe in miracles and in sainthood. I am not so arrogant as to scoff at these two eternal verities. Miracles I have witnessed—the dead raised, the mortally ill healed—all your standard supernatural fare. And the natural miracles too, such as what happened the time I ate a peach and threw the pit out the kitchen window. The next year, there grew a little peach tree from which a child of mine has since picked peaches to eat.

"As for sainthood, well, nobody said that it was something that dwelt within a man all his life, like his bones. Rather, it is intended for most people only once or twice in their lives, and then only for a moment or two. I applaud the democracy with which God dispenses holiness, having taken the bulk of it away from those few old men and young virgins in whom it formerly reposited, and spread it about among the rest of us, so that we, each of us, Jew and Gentile, priest and prostitute, can count on being graced by at least one shaft of it before we die. One shaft of grace...But that's enough. For in that moment, It is given to us to know Love."[1]

"So far then we have seen that, through our Lord Jesus Christ, by faith we are judged righteous and at peace with God, since it is by faith and through Jesus that we have entered this state of grace in which we can boast about looking forward to God's glory." Romans 5:1,2

The potential for love is limitless and so are the barriers to giving and receiving love. Perhaps one of the greatest enemies of love taking place in congregations and communities of all kinds is the misplaced deeds of those who defeat that which they say they represent. The congregation of those who walked out of church and synagogue never to return because of the action of priest, minister, or rabbi, and a host of lay people, is a larger congregation than any of us would like to admit.

God's grace and our love for one another are not hindered by the mess that some "religious" folk make, unless it is by our own permission. Each day is a struggle to gain clarity about what God is doing and not doing;

what he thinks of us and what he does not think of us—and to maintain that clarity while contradictory claims come from those who should know better.

How difficult and costly to humans is the misplaced word and deed done in the name of religion! To know the difference between good faith and bad religion is the daily struggle that belongs to us.

———

[1]Richard Selzer, *Confessions of a Knife* (New York: Simon and Schuster, 1979), p. 90.

"Eight days later the disciples were in the house again and Thomas was with them. The doors were closed, but Jesus came in and stood among them." John 20:26

So, here we are, freshly hit by the ancient invitation to choose life when many lesser options are open. Life open to our choosing is what is given; life locked in is what is claimed. Of course we could get our psych books out and offer reason upon reason for our choosing the locked-in life. But we are meditating in the middle of the night—the hour of our life-questioning demands a bottom line, no frills meeting of life's puzzles against its possibilities.

We must give in to the fact that **most of the things we claim to be victims of, are exactly those things chosen by us in life, and having the chance again, we would choose the same again.** Life would be so much better, if we could just claim our predicaments as **ours**—and go on from there, instead of spending the rest of our lives claiming to be victims of some choice that is no one's but ours.

The popularity of Colleen McCullough's saga, *The Thorn Birds*, transfixed many as the lives of a few were paraded across pages and then the screen. The legend that marks the beginning of the story is one of a bird that sings only once as it casts its body on the sharpest thorn it can find. It sings more beautifully than anything. One song. Life itself the cost. At the end of the 500-page novel is this: "The bird with the thorn in its breast, it follows an immutable law; it is driven by it knows not what to impale itself, and die singing. At the very instant the thorn enters there is no awareness in it of the dying to come; it simply sings and sings until there is not the life left to utter another note. But we, when we put the thorns in our breast, we know. We understand. And still we do it. Still we do it."[2]

There are so many gaps in scripture that cause me to wonder. Those ten lepers cured by Jesus...I wonder about them. I mean, they were ill, and had adjusted life and its expecta-

which all is settled, but to a seeking and not finding, to the burning sense of loss in possession which only lovers know."[2]

------

[1]Robert Farrar Capon, *Hunting The Divine Fox* (New York: The Seabury Press, 1974), p. 42.
[2]Ibid., p. 41.

The Bottom Line

In Will Campbell's book, *Brother to a Dragonfly*, he speaks often of his brother, affectionately called P.D. P.D. is an alcoholic, among other things, and an antagonist to the Christian faith his brother Will represents as a minister. P.D. likes arguments. One day while driving along in the car, Will tells this story of the conversation he had with P.D. . . .

"

. . .and that was when he asked me to define the Christian Faith. But he had a way of pushing one for simple answers. 'Just tell me what this Jesus cat is all about. I'm not too bright but maybe I can get the hang of it.' The nearest I ever came to giving him a satisfactory answer was once when I blasted him for some childish 'can God make a rock so big He couldn't pick it up' criticism of the Faith. He blasted right back. 'Okay. If you would tell me what the hell the Christian Faith is all about maybe I wouldn't make an ass of myself when I'm talking about it. Keep it simple. In ten words or less, what's the Christian message?' We were going someplace, or coming back from someplace when he said, 'Let me have it. Ten words.' I said, **'We're all bastards but God loves us anyway.'** He swung his car off on the shoulder and stopped, asking me to say it again. I repeated: 'We're all bastards but God loves us anyway.' He didn't comment on what he thought about the summary except to say, after he had counted the number of words on his fingers, 'I gave you a ten word limit. If you want to try again you have two words left.' I didn't try again but he often reminded me of what I had said that day."[1]

"We were still helpless when at his appointed moment Christ died for sinful men...When we

were reconciled to God by the death of his Son,
we were still enemies; now that we have been re-
conciled, surely we may count on being saved by
the life of his Son? Not merely because we have
been reconciled but because we are filled with
joyful trust in God, through our Lord Jesus
Christ, through whom we have already gained
our reconciliation." Romans 5:6,10,11

After being bored by pop-psychology and pop-theology books, I began reading spiritual biographies; life stories that combine the best of good theological work, which we need, with everyday life stories, which we live. Of all the work of William Sloane Coffin, none has gained as much attention as the sermon he preached two weeks after his son was killed in an accident in Boston Harbor. Here a great preacher suddenly is called upon to give his spiritual biography in light of his son's untimely death. To speak from the mix of study, emotion, life, and death—to speak from the gut where the rubber meets the road is the kind of story that is needed in every age. Ours is no exception.

Instead, the church has spent an inordinate amount of time taking good news from the New Testament, and has put requirements and toll gates in front of what God has offered freely, by faith, in Jesus of Nazareth. Some have caught on, and perhaps that is why we have so many believers of good news on the streets instead of the pews. Some caught on that the good news freely proclaimed in Biblical word is not celebrated in the average parish. And they are right.

We need some bottom line faith statements, coupled with bottom line action and example. That kind of faith and life makes quantum leaps in affecting people for the better.

---

[1]Will Campbell, *Brother To A Dragonfly* (New York: Morrow and Co., 1980), p. 220.

Locking Yourself In

"   •••In a family of my acquaintance were two brothers, the younger of whom had a dread of open doors. The older one became impatient, as older brothers will be, and, wanting to break him of his habit, he threatened: 'One day I will lock you up in a room with all the doors open.' "[1]

Ernest Campbell wrote a sermon and book inspired by this story titled *Locked in a Room with Open Doors*. Campbell suggested that we lock ourselves in—we strangle life for ourselves through vengeance, worry, anxiety, and an endless list of self-sabatoging activities.

We often lock ourselves in by saying that we want to get well while, consciously or unconsciously, working continually toward our downfall. We go through the motions of wanting help, wanting to become well—and in fact we don't. William Glasser's *Reality Therapy* states: "Without denying that the patient had an unsatisfactory past, we find that to look for what went wrong does not help him. What good comes from discovering that you are afraid to assert yourself because you had a domineering father? Both patient and therapist can be aware of this historical occurrence; they can discuss it in all of its ramifications for years, but the knowledge will not help the patient assert himself now."

"...I set before you life or death, blessing or curse. Choose life, then, so that you and your descendants may live in the love of God...."
Deut. 30:19

"Eight days later the disciples were in the house again and Thomas was with them. The doors were closed, but Jesus came in and stood among them." John 20:26

So, here we are, freshly hit by the ancient invitation to choose life when many lesser options are open. Life open to our choosing is what is given; life locked in is what is claimed. Of course we could get our psych books out and offer reason upon reason for our choosing the locked-in life. But we are meditating in the middle of the night—the hour of our life-questioning demands a bottom line, no frills meeting of life's puzzles against its possibilities.

We must give in to the fact that **most of the things we claim to be victims of, are exactly those things chosen by us in life, and having the chance again, we would choose the same again.** Life would be so much better, if we could just claim our predicaments as **ours**—and go on from there, instead of spending the rest of our lives claiming to be victims of some choice that is no one's but ours.

The popularity of Colleen McCullough's saga, *The Thorn Birds*, transfixed many as the lives of a few were paraded across pages and then the screen. The legend that marks the beginning of the story is one of a bird that sings only once as it casts its body on the sharpest thorn it can find. It sings more beautifully than anything. One song. Life itself the cost. At the end of the 500-page novel is this: "The bird with the thorn in its breast, it follows an immutable law; it is driven by it knows not what to impale itself, and die singing. At the very instant the thorn enters there is no awareness in it of the dying to come; it simply sings and sings until there is not the life left to utter another note. But we, when we put the thorns in our breast, we know. We understand. And still we do it. Still we do it."[2]

There are so many gaps in scripture that cause me to wonder. Those ten lepers cured by Jesus. . .I wonder about them. I mean, they were ill, and had adjusted life and its expectations to being that way. Also, I'm not convinced by scripture that they adequately answered the question, **"Do you want to be healed?"** I'm sure that upon being healed they all set out to do exactly what they were doing before they contracted the dreaded disease. And how many of those, whose want to be healed we are unsure of, finally gave in to disease again, because they knew not how to live any other way?

So, we have a healer coming to people, with the chief question being, "do you want to be healed?" Far more truth about life lies in that question than we ever thought. And after having witnessed all his healings and miracles, Thomas insists that he will not buy the last miracle until he touches the one in question. After opening the door for many broken lives and calling those closest to him to faith, Jesus seeks to crash the door of doubt once more by moving through the door that kept him out. **That** not being enough for Thomas, the one in the room most like us, he must touch side and hands. "Ok, now I believe. It's you. For sure. I'm sure now."

Sure you're sure, friend Thomas. You were sure when he first called you. You were sure at your first witnessed miracle. You were sure the whole enterprise, brief and beautiful as it was, was over outside the Jerusalem wall. And you are just as sure now, that he—the one, is alive now, forever. And just as sure as you are now, you will daily doubt the power you have seen; the power that transforms human life. I mean, Tom, you—just like me, will **daily** choose between life and death, health and unhealth, and between believing and un-believing, no matter what you have seen or shared. We all share your room, Tom—the one locked with open doors.

------

[1]Hans Sachs, *Masks of Love and Life* (Cambridge, Mass.: Science-Art Publishers, 1948), p. 54.

[2]Colleen McCullough, *The Thorn Birds* (New York: Harper & Row, Publishers, 1977), p. 560.

What You Want
More Than Anything Else

In Frederick Buechner's book, *The Final Beast*, there is a young clergyman seeking to give counsel to a troubled woman in his parish. He is recently widowed, she married to a man who ignores her. The small town is suspect of the relationship between pastor and parishwoman. The woman is seeing a zaney spiritual advisor by the name of Lillian Flagg. Nicolet, the minister, seeks out this same spiritualist in order to get advice on what his next move should be with his parishioner. Lillian Flagg seeks to get him to come to terms with himself.

"

    • • •give her what she really wants, Nicolet."

"Give her what, for Christ's sake?"

"For Christ's sake. . ." Lillian Flagg took a deep breath, then let it out slowly, shaking her head. "The only thing you have to give." And then she almost shouted at him. "Forgive her for Christ's sake, little priest!"

"But she knows I forgive her."

"She doesn't know God forgives her. That's the only power you have—to tell her that. Not just that he forgives her the poor little adultery. But the faces she can't bear to look at now. The man's. Her husband's. Her own, half the time. Tell her he forgives her for being lonely and bored, for not being full of joy with a houseful of children. That's what sin really is. You know—not being full of joy. Tell her that sin is forgiven because whether she knows it or not, that's what she wants more than anything else—what all of us want. What on earth do you think you were ordained for?"[1]

"For this reason I tell you that her sins, her many sins, must have been forgiven her, or she would not have shown such great love. It is the

man who is forgiven little who shows little love." Then he said to her, "Your sins are forgiven." Luke 7:47,48

Oh, we see clearly now. It was too simple. Under our nose all the time. The one who loves little in life is the one that feels most unforgiven. Either the good word of forgiveness has not been given, or more often than not, the good word has been given and the person just can't accept that word in light of their mistakes and crimes. Or, perhaps the backward glances and whispers on main street keep the prison gate of condemnation in place.

We deny others the same grace we deny ourselves. How important it is to first allow that grace to touch us, and thereby allow ourselves to get on to the joy of living found in passing on the same.

The one who loves little, has accepted little forgiveness for themselves.

The one thing people need more than forgiveness from others is a knowledge that the one with whom they ultimately deal with, in fact, has forgiven them.

We deny grace to others to the same measure we deny it to ourselves.

---

[1]Frederick Buechner, *The Final Beast* (San Francisco: Harper & Row, Publishers, 1965), p. 174, 175.

Knowing Enough of God
To Want To Worship Him

"**I** know only enough of God to want to worship him, by any means ready to hand."

"There is one church here, so I go to it. On Sunday mornings I quit the house and wander down the hill to the white frame church in the firs. On a big Sunday there might be twenty of us there; often I am the only person under sixty, and feel as though I'm on an archaeological tour of Soviet Russia. The members are of mixed denominations; the minister is a Congregationalist, and wears a white shirt. The man knows God. Once, in the middle of the pastoral prayer of intercession for the whole world—for the gift of wisdom to its leaders, for hope and mercy to the grieving and pained, succor to the oppressed, and God's grace to all—in the middle of this he stopped, and burst out, 'Lord, we bring you these same petitions every week.' After a shocked pause, he continued reading the prayer. Because of this, I like him very much."

"The higher Christian churches—where, if anywhere, I belong—come at God with an unwarranted air of professionalism, with authority and pomp, as though they knew what they were doing, as though people in themselves were an appropriate set of creatures to have dealings with God. I often think of the set pieces of liturgy as certain words which people have successfully addressed to God without their getting killed. In the high churches they saunter through the liturgy like Mohawks along a strand of scaffolding who have long since forgotten their danger. If God were to blast such a service to bits, the congregation would be, I believe, genuinely shocked. But in the low churches you expect it any minute. This is the beginning of wisdom."[1]

"But Jesus answered him, 'Scripture says: You must worship the Lord your God, and serve him alone.' " Mathew 4:10

I'd say 90 percent of all weddings and funerals I do are for people outside the congregation. One learns early about a common speech that comes up by the couple to be married, or from the family of the deceased. "Daddy didn't go to church for 30 years, but really believed, even prayed every night, and the reason he didn't go is because that hypocrite minister ran off with the organist way back when and daddy didn't want to be a part of that group—but he believed, Reverend, and he was a **good** man—and loved the outdoors. Please say that in the service." The conversation varies with a couple getting married. Because they like the preacher they say that they are going to be coming to church every Sunday right after they return from their honeymoon. They say that because I'm nice and they think that is what I want them to say. They never show up. I know that and they know that in the exact moment they make their pledge of attendance. Spare me.

Our galloping Gallup pollsters tell us that 95 percent of the people interviewed on the street believe in God. Of those, 89 percent pray anywhere from a little, to a lot. However, only 33 percent of all those find their way to a church or synagogue on a given week.

I speak in defense of those who don't go. Most often the private faith I hear people voicing to me has a far more forgiving, loving and caring God than the one portrayed in most churches. Too often the less involved in a local congregation, the more loving is their image of God. Of course I think faith is far more enhanced by being a part of a loving community that meets often to mingle love, laughter, tears and fears together around a communion table. Good examples of such congregations are fewer than I would like to admit.

I rejoice, that, midst troubled experiences in congregations, God's grace gets scattered, somehow, so that most of those on the street can know enough to want to worship him anyway, in private or public.

---

[1]Annie Dillard, *Holy The Firm* (New York: Harper & Row, Publishers, 1977), p. 55, 57, 59.

'I'm So Glad It's Like That'

It was hot and we were late getting to Love Center in Oakland. I discovered that being late is not a problem because I never figured out when we started. Anyway, the worship kept starting for 30 minutes with all kinds of singing—joyful sounds, I tell you.

The minister was gone that day. Then the announcement came that the associate minister was gone. Then we heard the good news that one of the eight lay ministers would speak, and this day it was a woman whose name I don't know.

"I'm going to talk about the banquet of the Lord," she began. "Now when we talk about the banquet of the Lord, we ain't talkin' bout no junk food. There ain't no Dorritoes! There ain't no Ho Ho's! There ain't no Twinkies! There ain't no Ding Dongs at the Table of the Lord! At HIS banquet, we get prime rib! I want to talk about that."

Right then I knew I wasn't in for any main-line-protestant-sit-proper-in-your-seat-three-piece-suit kind of sermon. In fact, as she took the next step and quickly dismissed any exegesis and interpretation made of her passage (from Song of Songs), and declared most of seminary hoopla to miss the point, I knew she and I were going to be friends.

"His banner over me is Love," she quoted from Song of Songs. She told of Solomon and his many loves, and the erotic nature of the text and told us not to get bogged down nor ignore the lustful nature of the text. She declared that Solomon had this special love relationship, a woman he brings into the banquet hall with him, where others know of her special place in his life: "for his banner over me is love."

Then she said, "that's the way it is with us before God." In spite of all we have been and in spite of all we have done, in spite of everything, his banner over us is love. **"And I'm so glad it's like that."**

And I'm so glad that I had the chance to hear this woman (I must find her name). "You white folks," she said after we hugged and talked, "paint your theological pictures with your checkbooks. We black folk paint only with the stories of faith."

I liked her very much. I'm so glad that God's grace is just like she painted that day.

"It was before the festival of the Passover, and Jesus knew that the hour had come for him to pass from this world to the Father. He had always loved those who were his in the world, but NOW he showed how perfect his love was."
John 13:1

Border Song

Workcamps among the poor have odd reversals. Those who come to help are the benefactors, not the ones the work is done for. Why is it that I have never been more deeply moved than when being given the privilege to work among the poor?

One such workcamp involved 70 people going by bus to a village in Northern Mexico, in the state of Sonora called Oquitoa. The village is like so many—poor, about 600 population, basic income is from agriculture. We church folk of protestant bent came to work among our Catholic brothers and sisters by painting with them their local school. If it were just to get the work done, we would not go and they would not invite us. But, for the beauty of being together, they invited us and we went.

Holy week was the week we shared. Thursday came and it was time for us to share our traditional Maunday Thursday service. Bread was plentiful in the village. We bought some. Welch's grapejuice was unheard of, and besides, what a joke to our Catholic friends that we should still be taking communion cleansed by prohibition. Wine came forth, from a woman who makes her own from some berry that is not plentiful. Her last bottle was ours. We broke bread, and drank wine around an altar complete with paintbrushes, paint cans and other symbols of our being together with these good people. But what a sham I thought. The ones we come to be with and share life with are not with us at this holy table. Sure, different language. Sure, different background under the Christian umbrella.

But here are the greatest symbols of reconciliation and togetherness and we just aren't together. We celebrated, embraced, ate, drank, prayed, went quietly to tents. Our service was incomplete. For me at least.

Good Friday came. Our last morning and I went to the top of a hill where a 450-year-old whitewashed church stood. I was wanting to catch the sunrise splashing on the church and dry surroundings. As I approached the church, I discovered that I was not alone. A woman stood on the porch nodding kindly. I have found that when people can't communicate by language, they end up smiling and nodding a lot. We did. She turned out to be the woman who brought us the wine! I finally recognized her. We nodded more, smiled more. She broke the silence by mixing a little English and Spanish. "Senor, many religions; but UNO DIOS!" There are many religions, but one God! In that instant, the communion service begun the night before was finally complete. Old woman, poor, wrinkled and toothlessly delightful, shares with young seminary student a truth that he had better not lose while reading thick books—we belong together, no matter how much we are separated by language, age, nationality and geography.

It was a Good Friday after all.

"She has done what was in her power to do. . .I tell you solemnly, wherever throughout all the world the Good News is proclaimed, what she has done will be told also. . . ." Mark 14:8,9

Same Border, Another Verse

Mike Yard, the minister I am pleased to work with, tra-
veled with our high school youth and sponsors to Ti-
juana, Baja, Mexico to work. One special project involved helping people who live at the town dump—
assisting them to put concrete slabs under the houses so
they will not be washed away at the time of the rains.
On the last day at the dump, our visiting youth and the
Mexican workers joined together for the last day's
work. Mike tells what happened...

"**W**e gathered for lunch. My work party
told me they could not eat without sharing, so
we distributed one sandwich to each worker,
then approached the children, offering them
each a sandwich as well. We also had one

orange for each of our workers, and the oranges were given to the children of the dump. As we gave them the food, I asked Jennie to explain that they had to eat inside. If they took the food out, we would be surrounded by people, and we had barely enough for those who were inside. They agreed, and began to eat with one exception. Maria didn't eat. Her eyes are the eyes of an adult many years older, filled with the compassion and wisdom of suffering. She refused the sandwich until I pleaded with her to take it. 'Please, we are amigos.' She finally gave in and accepted it and hugged me for a long, long time. I looked into these eyes and became confused, unsure of who had been the giver, and who the recipient. I had given her food, she had given me something much more difficult to define or understand, but I had a sense of having received a valuable gift.

"Maria went off to the corner with her sandwich and orange, and sat waiting as we all finished eating, then moved toward the door. We stopped her, again explaining that she could not take the sandwich out of the building. Her eyes took on an authority which we could not challenge as she explained, 'It is for my sister.' "

"...*taken for paupers though we make others rich, for people having nothing though we have everything.*" II Cor. 6:10b

We need to sing the border song often. Why? For some unknown reason the road to the sacred necessarily passes by the way of poor folk who have lessons for us about life. We come to them among the three percent wealthy of the world, from a country whose people have proven that you can have every material item and still be unhappy.

As always, the gift bearers receive the gift—the gift of new perspective.

He'll Be There Then
And He's There Now!

Listening to a student read the Scripture in seminary chapel, Joseph Sittler, now blind, heard something he's never heard before. "Yea, though I walk through the valley of the shadow of death, I will fear no evil, for Thou art with me."

"The text does not speak," said Sittler, "of the valley of death but of the valley of the shadow of death. There is a difference. The valley of death is an experience through which we walk from this life unto the life to come. To be sure, God will be with us as we walk through that valley. What appears in Psalm 23, however, is not a portrayal of the death experience and God's promised presence in it. Rather, the psalm suggests that even while we live, the assured future arrival of death casts a shadow over us. It is as if this life tilts forward toward death; we walk in a valley now, the shadow of death covering our paths even before the experience of death comes.

"The wonderful truth captured by that hearing of the passage is that God is with us now. It is not simply that God will be with us in the experience of death itself; it is that God will walk with us through all of life, a life over which death sometimes casts its shadow."[1]

". . .it is all that is good, everything that is perfect, which is given us from above; it comes down from the Father of all light; with him there is no such thing as alteration, no shadow of a change." James 1:17

The church has been entrusted with a book that we call THE book. In this book is not THE word, but many words. And these words are different words and they fit different occasions. I liked the description that the Bible is like a box of flashlights, each being brought out at the right moment to shed some light on whatever problem is before us. We have this depository of different words—each word speaking to us at the moment we need that word most.

In my younger days I was anxious to be "right" and make sure to get the world to line up in agreement with what I had to say. I was, to greater or lesser degree, out to change the world. The youthful word was mixed with anger about the injustices of this world. That anger is well founded in biblical stories. Now, another word emerges. At midlife, I have friends who are dying at my age. Suddenly the angry, marching orders that led us to the streets for social justice have been replaced, at least for the moment, with a different Biblical word that rings true to the present experience: "even though I walk through the valley of the shadow— I fear no evil, for you are with me."

We faith-seeking people are trustees of words and THE word. And most of our task is to know what word is appropriate at a specific time, and to know how to pull that word into view until shadows fade to light, and doubt gives way to better questions.

---

[1]Quoted by Martin Marty in *Context*, August 1 and 15, 1984.

57 Reasons Not to Have a Nuclear War, And Don't Forget My Etching!

Marty Asher and Lonni Sue Johnson teamed up and put together a picture book. In pictures they show 57 reasons not to have a nuclear war including cheese, Friday afternoons, ice cream, soap, almonds and Lena Horne, just to mention a few. You get the drift. The final reasons not to have such a war are you, and me.

And don't forget my etching, I would hasten to add. The one by Claus Sievert with a small clown sitting on a piano, with Mahler's 9th Symphony sitting there too. I bought it because I had no choice. Have you seen that one piece of art that you know, by first glance, somehow, you have been looking for all your life. I would lose that etching, and the sight of it, and its meaning to me—I would like to make that 58 reasons not to have a nuclear war. I like my etching.

In *The Clowns of God* by Morris West, a poetic moment comes when the defrocked pope, now playing the role of a clown as an alternative way of waking the world up to impending nuclear doom, becomes eloquent in a letter he directs to God: "When a man becomes a clown he makes a free gift of himself to the audience. To endow them with the saving grace of laughter, he submits to be mocked, drenched, clouted, crossed in love. Your Son made the same submission when He was crowned as a mock king, and the troops spat wine and water in His face. . .My hope is that when He comes again, He will still be human enough to shed a clown's gentle tears over the broken toys—that once were women and children."[1]

When Jesus said, "Let the children come to me and don't hinder them," his reason for allowing them center stage is because they can often see better than adults who have had more years to suppress their deepest longings and highest ideals. Willingly, or unwillingly, we become blind to that which we should not. Adults speak of nuclear war and more weapons in the same manner and urgency that I say to you, "please pass the salt" over breakfast. But given the simple facts—that we have enough big bombs to wipe out the earth and my clown etching 50 times over—give that simple fact to a child and they can easily tell you—"that could ruin your whole day, life, earth—forever. Don't do it."

May we all get that simple enough soon, in order to save ourselves.

---

[1]Morris West, *The Clowns of God* (New York: William Morrow and Company, Inc., 1981), p. 222, 223.

Walk Well

"Frederick S. Peris, the founder of Gestalt therapy, was a master showman. He was also a master craftsman. (He believed) that the presence of a group or even a large audience is necessary, for one thing, to keep the therapist honest. Thousands of people watched him work, and his sessions were recorded on hundreds of hours of tape, video tape and film before his death in 1970. Those in the audience could see, in a few minutes, just how much a person loves his neurosis, how desperately he clings to it, how cunningly he manipulates the environment to keep it propped up, how he will resort to charm, humor, intelligence, deafness, blindness, dumbness, confusion, pity, outrage, amnesia, *anything* to avoid the loss of this, his most precious possession, his adored dis-ease."[1]

"Do you want to be healed?" John 5:6

Early ministry was difficult in one way. I thought the roles were clear: You bring me your hurt, and I bring you my help. Easy enough. Roles are clear. Then I scratched my head for ten years during many counseling sessions, realizing that just as soon as we cleared up a big problem in this person desiring help, by golly they pulled another out of the bag and brought that in. Or if they didn't have one in the bag, they would create one. Something was missing in my understanding of the nature of giving and receiving help, until I was helped by this quote from George Leonard.

I likewise was not among those who found a lot of things in the New Testament that I was sure did not come out of the mouth of Jesus. I felt I never knew enough to say that. However, I did think one item didn't belong. When Jesus would approach some poor sucker who had been sick for 37 years, I thought it was absurd for him to ask, "Do you want to be healed?" That which I thought did not belong, in fact stands as Jesus' wisdom at its greatest. If that guy didn't want to be healed, Jesus could zap all the magic into him and make him whole only to find him sick by midnight—all because that man didn't want to be well. Sickness is good for having a permanent excuse for not taking responsibility for your life. What is discovered, far too late, is that the pain of our sickness is greater than the pain we thought would be there when taking daily responsibility for ourselves.

When I was in Jamaica, I liked their greeting much like our salutation "take care of yourself." When departing they say, "Walk well!" More often than not, more often than we are aware, being well is a choice more than a chance.

[1]George Leonard, *The Transformation* (New York: Dell Publishing Co., Inc., 1972), p. 72.

"The Clowns of God"

Jean Marie Barette is Pope. He has a vision much like that in the Revelation of St. John, about the impending end of the world about to come. His Cardinals think he's mad, and Jean Marie decides to step down. Among his travels as a common priest, he is in a park at early evening. A woman is watching a group of neatly dressed children and is embroidering.

"As Jean Marie passed along the gravelled walk, one of the children broke away from the group and ran towards him. She slipped on the verge and fell almost at his feet. She burst into tears. He picked her up and carried her to the woman on the bench, who dabbed at her grazed knee and offered her a lollipop to soothe her. It was only then that Jean Marie noticed that the child was a mongol—as indeed were all the others in the group. As if sensing his shock, the woman held the child towards him and said with a smile:

" 'We are all from the Institute across the road...This one has just come to us. She's homesick; so she thinks every man is her papa.'

" 'And where is Papa?' There was a touch of censure in the question.

"The woman shook her head. 'Oh, no, it isn't what you think. He's been recently widowed. He feels, quite rightly, that she is safer here with us...We have about a hundred children in the Institute. The *patronne* lets us bring the little ones here to play. Her only child was mongoloid but it died early.'

"Jean Marie held out his arms. The child came to him willingly and kissed him, then sat in his lap and began playing happily with the buttons of his shirt.

" 'How do you maintain the Institute?'

" 'We have a grant from the government. We ask fees from parents who can pay. We solicit private charity. Fortunately we have some wealthy sponsors like Monsieur Duhamel, who lives close by. He calls the children *les petites bouffonnes du bon Dieu*. . .God's little clowns. . . .'

" 'It's a gentle thought.' "[1]

"Blessed are the pure in heart, for they shall see God." Matthew 5:8

I remember an early Monday morning—the day after Easter. I was still in a daze over the busting-out-of-the-tomb celebration the day before. Why can't life always be just like that great day? Anyway, I had to fight the freeway for two hours to get to San Francisco International Airport to pick up Jon. He had been away for a week visiting relatives. Jon is mentally retarded. In comparison to other Down's-syndrome youth, his condition is not too severe.

Out of the gate (20 minutes late—which is normal and lucky for the day after Easter!)

came Jon with a beautiful stewardess to deliver him to Dad. He handed me the papers that parents and relatives sign when sending a child alone on the plane. I noted the caption on the top—a word to anyone who might seek to assist Jon: *Note: This child is retarted.* I laughed and thought of life's reversals—I mean even Jon can spell *retarded*!

Then while waiting for luggage I turned around to find Jon lying on the inclined baggage carousel—taking a ride. By the way he was settled in among the luggage, I would guess it was his fourth trip around when I caught him. He received his parental instructions. He promised never, ever to do it again. Why do I doubt youthful oaths like these?

We finally got the baggage. The sky cap assisted Jon and gave him the gifts of a smile and a warm southern-drawl greeting. Jon explained where he had been. The skycap vanished into the crowd. While walking toward the door, Jon informs me that he must find his friend for a moment. Jon hustles through the crowd and finds his friend and hands him the best Easter egg in his basket Dad was holding. The sky cap is grateful. Jon is aglow. I see Easter all over again in their eyes.

Easter is more than a day and more than a season. Easter was intended to be every day, and it is for those with good eyes. For, with proper vision, you can see life creeping out of small places and singing out a song: "death will not have the last word with us."

On the freeway heading home, thinking of writing about this good day in a book of meditations someday, my sometimes angelic son smiles, and empties his pockets on the seat and is proud that he was able to cram into his pockets some 20 little bars of soap that he found in a very small restroom on the plane! Cancel the angelic comment! He is nothing different, or special. He is just like us, only more honest about it—saint and shadow blended beneath an Easter smile.

So, I will write meditations after writing this—"Dear Air Cal: You don't know me, but as a minister I could be in trouble if I don't let you know that I know you've been missing some soap lately. You see, my son. . . ."

---

[1]Morris West, *The Clowns of God* (New York: William Morrow and Company, Inc., 1981), p. 222, 223.

Why Bother Trying
When I Know I Will Fail?

"

• • • love is the power to live gladly as imperfect lovers. Not only is love the power to forget oneself in concern for others, it is also the power to forgive oneself for not forgetting oneself. This power is the love of God for us in the form of crucified love, the love we discover when we see Christ's cross as God's entrance into our lives with a love that forgives *all*. When we have the power to accept his love, we have the power to accept ourselves gladly as weak persons who cannot easily manage to love as God loves us.

"In the courage born of accepting love, we can look love's ideal full in the face, admit we do not measure up to it, and yet yield ourselves again and again to love as the power that pushes us very gradually toward it. With this courage, we can cope with the unending job of finding our way through the complex network of our duties, demands, and drives, through life's crisscrossing desires and needs, toward a life increasingly disposed to love others without demanding a return on our investment."[1]

"And because wickedness is multiplied, most people's love will grow cold." Matthew 24:12

I make no fun of my Sunday School upbringing when I tell you this. I remember countless times that well-intended lessons all found a common dead end. "What is a Christian?" would be the question. The answer would undoubtedly be "One who follows Jesus." Then it was made clear that we all had to be like Jesus. As early as second grade, folks, I knew we were in for trouble if in fact that is our goal. Look the Christian ideal in the eye and, shazam!, it's obvious that I am not going to come close to measuring up to it. Then why bother looking? Why bother trying? What is our hope?

First, by daring to look and admitting how far we fail, something happens, in that we are nudged toward love's goal without being conscious of that.

Second, we must first of all allow ourselves to be benefactors of this great love before we can have any hope of the same love being brokered through us.

Scott Peck helped us all in his book, *The Road Less Travelled,* and later in *People of the Lie.* Scott says there is a part of every one of us that belongs in jail! The presence of evil is mysterious and real. The only hope for my controlling that shadow part of myself is to admit its existence and dare to look at it. To the degree that we look is to the degree that the shadow side can be held in check. By denying its existence, that shadow side runs us.

So, why try to love in some way imitative of the Christ, when in advance I know that I will fail? The answer is—stop trying. Dare to look love's ideal in the face with the full knowledge of your inability to live up to it—and, by telling the truth about that, somehow, by looking long enough and often enough, you will be nudged again and again toward that loving way.

---

[1]Lewis B. Smedes, *Love Within Limits* (Grand Rapids: Wm. B. Erdmans Publishing Co., 1978), p. 134, 135.

Listening to the Voice Outside

"**I** propose that theologians write theology from the standpoint of the mother in Bombay (or Pittsburgh) whose child has just starved to death. She would not be theology's primary reader, and her situation would not provide theology's subject matter. Her rage and grief would provide its angle of vision. From there let the theologian write about God, Jesus Christ, revelation, holy history, new pluralism, living word, love, loving plan, righteousness, church, justice, liberation, the sacraments, self-transcending authenticity, religious experience, possibilities for existence, the Christian triumph over evil, and the resurrection. A theology written from that standpoint would have ceased being a problem to itself."[1]

"So Pharaoh summoned Abram and said, 'What is this you have done to me? Why did you not tell me she was your wife? Why did you say, 'She is my sister,' so that I took her for my wife? Now, here is your wife. Take her and go!'"
Genesis 12:18-20

You know the story. Abram is heading to Egypt because of famine. His wife is good looking. He is afraid that the king will kill him and take her for another of his wives. Abram works it out—he asks Sarah to pretend that she is his sister. Pharoah discovers that he has taken for his wife a woman who belongs to another. Abram is brought before Pharoah, chastised and given a lecture on social ethics by the king. The king returns Abram's wife and a moral lesson all at the same time.

The Claremont scholar, James Sanders, reminds us that the first lecture on ethics in the Bible comes from a heathen king, one who stands completely outside the Hebrew faith, outside the chosen people. It is very important to listen to voices outside our circle. Often it is the voice that calls us to the faith we say we profess.

Ron is outside. Ron is a street man who is dependent upon our congregation's food pantry handouts in order to live. He lives outside and apparently doesn't want it any other way. Many have tried to get him off the streets. That effort has failed. Ron is outside his mind also. He is not mentally well. Something is missing; I don't know what. He is outside and often comes in. When it is too cold, he is there first thing in the morning for coffee. He gets four good smiles, free coffee and for a few moments Ron's world is not so cruel. He gets his food for the day or week. He doesn't say much. Sometimes he shows up for worship and will not sit anywhere else but the back row. He came on Christmas eve and allowed us to pay his room for the night—the night we remembered one who didn't have such luck. Ron blessed us by allowing us to exercise our intolerance for him being on the street that night. He graced us as we feared making the same mistake of a Bethlehem motel. "Thanks," he said.

Once he had a penny he wanted to give a little girl. The coffee hour was going after worship and a rare beauty five years of age was beaming in the midst of a happy day. Ron came to me to show me the penny and get my permission to give it to this little girl. He gave me a long lecture about trusting people to be with children and how he wanted me to know that the gift he seeks to give is safe. I remember his parched and dirty hand reaching out to this little girl who said "thank you." For one fleeting moment in time, the gulf between all that life should be and good intentions unfulfilled, touched. And smiles greeted each other. And each hurriedly ran back to their individual worlds—worlds miles apart except in the Eternal mind.

The one "outside" saves us inside the congregation weekly from forgetting to whom the kingdom is promised most.

---

[1]John B. Fry, *The Great Apostolic Blunder Machine* (San Francisco: Harper & Row, Publishers, 1978), p. 174, 175.

Hamburgers:
Sure Sign of Acceptance

Shortly after his grandmother died, Michael Yard, Associate Minister, gave this communion meditation at First Christian Church of Concord, California.

My grandmother died recently, and it really wasn't so much a time of sorrow as a time of reminiscence. I spent a couple of days lost in daydreams—remembering moments of closeness, of laughter, of warmth. I was surprised to find that I really couldn't remember any heavy conversations which we had ever shared—only short talks about the weather, and about what I was doing, how I liked my job, how she was doing on her diet. My grandmother never really had much to say; mostly she listened, and maybe answered a question or two while she went about her work in the kitchen.

It's the work in the kitchen that I remember most. When I worked at the swimming pool, teaching lessons and occasionally lifeguarding, I walked right by her house, and it seemed so natural to stop by for something to eat. So naturally I stopped. Often. And she never talked much, but she always fed me cheeseburgers and french fries.

Then came my rebellious years when I got caught up in the prevalent attitudes of the 60's, and grew long hair, started experimenting with drugs, wrote an underground newspaper, and got kicked out of high school. I was filled with anger at the injustice of the world, and I rebelled against everything and everyone. My memories of adults during those years are mostly memories of confrontation, of lectures, of shouting. But my grandmother still didn't talk much. I stopped by several times each week, and she never seemed to notice the long hair, the glassy eyes, the anger. At my grandmother's house—and only at grandmother's house—it was okay to still be a child. As for me, it was hard to find anything to rebel against in someone who fed me cheeseburgers and french fries.

Years later I settled down, went to college, entered the ministry. And I returned to my home town where I served as Associate Minister of the Christian Church. I was the prodigal son come home. People all seemed so proud of me, so impressed by me. As I remember I was pretty impressed with myself! I stopped by one afternoon to see my grandmother, to let her know that I had survived those rebellious years, that I was alright. I stopped by to impress her, hair cut, new suit and tie—if anyone had a right to be proud of me, she did. Grandma never did talk too much. As I entered, proud and dignified, she headed for the kitchen. She didn't seem to notice the haircut. She was unimpressed by the college degree.

Titles meant nothing to her. What really mattered was that I liked cheeseburgers and french fries.

I wasn't hungry, but I ate. Three cheeseburgers and a huge pile of french fries. It was more than food. It was always much more than food which she gave me. I knew of no way—I still know of no way I could have turned down these special cheeseburgers and french fries. They were cheeseburgers consecrated by a grandmother's love. Every bite communicated an unconditional love which she could never have said, nor could I have accepted so easily had our relationship been limited to words.

I am the living bread which has come down from heaven. Anyone who eats this bread will live forever;..." John 6:51a

Backroads

"The Hopi (Indian) believes mankind has evolved through four worlds: the first a shadowy realm of contentment; the second a place so comfortable the people forgot where they had come from and began worshipping material goods. The third world was a pleasant land too, but the people, bewildered by their past and fearful for their future, thought only of their own earthly plans. At last, the Spider Grandmother, who oversees the emergencies, told them: 'You have forgotten what you should have remembered, and now you have to leave this place. Things will be harder.' In the fourth and present world, life is difficult for mankind, and he struggles to remember his source because materialism and selfishness block a greater vision. The newly born infant comes into the fourth world with the door of his mind open (evident in the cranial soft spot), but as he ages, the door closes and he must work at remaining receptive to the great forces. A human being's grandest task is to keep from breaking with things outside himself."[1]

"They were on the road, going up to Jerusalem; Jesus was walking on ahead of them; they were in a daze, and those who followed were apprehensive." Mark 10:32a

Heat Moon, facing a divorce, jumped in a van and followed only blue highways (you know, the little backroads on your map where there isn't much traffic and a lot of good scenery). His name, William Least Heat Moon, was derived from his part Indian ancestry.

Jesus, likewise, took the backroads of his day, seeking to give higher happiness by pointing to a Kingdom not of this world. That back road was uphill. Still is. And his followers then are like us—in a daze and apprehensive of where on earth this wonder-of-God will lead us.

Indeed, we are a part of the Hopi fourth world—the one that struggles to remember the source because materialism and selfishness block a higher vision. We are a part of the world Jesus wept over— "Would this day that you knew what makes for peace; but right now it is hidden from your eyes."

May we be blessed with the right blue highway, that will get us off the main thoroughfares, where bright lights blind us— and may we be led to greater peace found on the road less travelled.

---

[1]William Least Heat Moon, *Blue Highways* (Boston: Little, Brown and Company, 1982), p. 192.

Be Kind, Please!

Eliot Rosewater, drunk, volunteer fireman, and President of the fabulously rich Rosewater Foundation is a slightly insane man. He is also filled with total love for humanity and is tormented by a maddeningly sane vision of society. Eliot has customarily sent a share of IBM stock to each new baby born in the county. In one moment of inspiration he thinks of a greeting to give to all babies being born into the world.

"**H**ello, babies. Welcome to Earth. It's hot in the summer and cold in the winter. It's round and wet and crowded. At the outside, babies, you've got about a hundred years here. There's only one rule that I know of, babies—:

"God damn it, you've got to be kind."[1]

". . .and be kind to one another, tenderhearted, forgiving one another,. . . ." Ephesians 4:32

Someone said that the mind is a marvelous instrument. Unfortunately, it did not come with instructions. We could say the same for life. All of life. And the more we miss the key to living a full life, the more people invent guide books that tell us how to "find life."

I can't stand it when people in politics, religion or classroom of any kind seek to make the complex simple. There are no simple solutions to many problems, and simple answers only add to the complexity of the problem. However, there are key principles in life, that were we to pay attention to, we would open up greater life for ourselves and others around us.

I remember the morning in the early 1950's that the old woodframe church I was growing up in, burnt to the ground. It was a shock to me. I somehow connected God as living there and rapidly needed to develop a new theology—all this at eight years of age. The fire was so devastating that everything was lost. They tried to pull out some old hymnals with watermarks. But everytime you opened one, you would get smoke smell. All was lost...except a marble plaque. My mother tried to get me to remember where it was placed in the old church, but my youthful mind hadn't paid enough attention to that detail. The plaque became the only thing that was salvaged from the old church—and was placed just at the entrance of the new church built several years later. It's inscription: "LOVE ONE ANOTHER." Every time I see that plaque now, all church history flashes by my face. Through the rubble of all the lynchings, wars, madness and witchhunts, judgments, errors and evils—and midst all of the church's victories for the good—if midst all that we could retrieve just one thing from the ashes of time—and that one thing was LOVE ONE ANOTHER—it would be enough! "See what love they have for each other." It would be enough to describe the church at its moments best, and the highest of purposes given the church in the young one from Nazareth. Simple. And enough. And **if we really lived that way**, it would be enough. Enough to discover fire for the second time.

An Eastern mystic was quoted as saying: "Love one another; be kind to one another. And if you can't do either, at least do no harm." Simple. Of course. If it were complex, we could hide behind its complexity and claim inability to live that way because we "just don't understand." But because it's so simple and clear, we ignore it.

Be kind, please. It's just better that way!

---

[1]Kurt Vonnegut, Jr., *God Bless You, Mr. Rosewater* (New York: Deli Publishing Co., Inc., 1965), p. 93.

Those Who Serve a Cause

"Those who serve a cause are not those who love the cause. They love the life they have to live in order to serve it. Except for the very purest, and they are rare. For the idea of a cause does not supply the necessary energy for serving it." —Simone Weil

"I don't know what your destiny will be; but one thing I know— The only ones among you who will be really happy are those who have sought and found how to serve." —Albert Schweitzer

"No longer do I call you servants, but friends."
—*Jesus*

We need clarity about service. Simone Weil punctures any preconception we might have that we serve out of our own generosity, with no sense of self-fulfillment desired. If you are Jesus or close to his kind, you probably can. If you are like the rest of us, there is more to be considered. How many servants in all kinds of professions have you seen "burn-out" after a short time at the job. Lawyers in ghettos, nurses in drug drop-in centers, clergy in impoverished places. When burn-out comes while serving the finest of causes for God and humanity, guilt pervades. Weil gives new clarity to the dilemma—ideas never supply the energy for serving even the finest of causes.

Schweitzer would never argue from a non-selfish standpoint. After several doctorates and still not finding fulfillment, he headed for another doctorate, this time in medicine and ended up in remote Africa. Happiness he found in serving in this way. He never wanted to draw attention to himself because he knew that his deepest need was being served when he was allowed to serve.

Process Theologian John B. Cobb, Jr., from Claremont, urges ministers to recover themselves for ministry. What does such a minister look like? They are strengthened by their own self identity; they have freedom that comes from greater self-responsibility; they recognize great possibilities for being choicemakers.

Paul Scherer said in the Lyman Beecher Lectures at Yale: "To have a mind of your own is to be another chance for the Kingdom in the hands of God; to have no mind but your own is to be no more than the ghost of that chance forever."

On Not Knowing
What Help Is Needed

In his fine novel, *A River Runs Through It*, Norman Maclean tells the story of a minister and his two sons and their two religions: Biblical faith and fly fishing. In one part of the story he tells of a younger son who is alcoholic. The older son and father discuss ways they can help the alcoholic son and brother, who really is not looking for help.

"You are too young to help anybody and I am too old," said the father. "By help I don't mean a courtesy like serving choke-cherry jelly or giving money."

"Help," he said, "is giving part of yourself to somebody who comes to accept it willingly and needs it badly."

"So it is," he said, using an old homiletic transition, "that we can seldom help anybody. Either we don't know what part to give or maybe we don't like to give any part of ourselves. Then, more often than not, the part that is needed is not wanted. And even more often, we do not have the part that is needed. It is like the auto-supply shop over town where they always say, 'Sorry, we are just out of that part.' "

I told him, "You make it too tough. Help doesn't have to be anything that big."

He asked me, "Do you think your mother helps him by buttering his rolls?"

"She might," I told him. "In fact, yes, I think she does."

"Do you think you help him?" he asked me.

"I try to," I said. "My trouble is I don't know him. In fact, one of my troubles is that I don't even know whether he needs help. I don't know, that's my trouble."

"That should have been my text," my father said. "We are willing to help, Lord, but what if anything is needed?"[1]

"Let us be confident, then, in approaching the throne of grace, that we shall have mercy from him and find grace when we are in need of help." Hebrews 4:16

Most of what we call help isn't any help at all. Rearranging deck chairs on our psychological ship is most often what we engage in when we speak of help. Several fallacies about getting help are these: (1) thinking that once you identify why you are the way you are, you will change. False. We have discovered that you can know all that stuff and still not be changed for the better. (2) We have also been naive when speaking of change. We unique beings have certain attitudes and values that have been programmed into us from birth. Those items are not simply or casually altered.

Morris Massey in speaking of this phenomenon has shown that what we are "gut-level" programmed with at a median age of ten is what you will carry throughout your life—UNLESS you have a significant emotional experience that changes that value or attitude. An example: let us assume that you have been told from birth that Vietnamese people smell and are not as bright as anglos. This attitude was taught and nurtured within your family circle. Then one day you head off to college and a young man by the name of Quan Ti is your roommate. After the first week you have discovered that he does not smell and that in fact he has helped you with your advanced triginometry and at the semester's end, he got far better grades than yourself. That is a significant emotional experience. Values are changed in the midst of this new framework of experience. How we seek or create significant emotional experiences is no simple matter.

Perhaps we can carve in stone these very true words: *"Help is giving part of yourself to somebody who comes to accept it willingly and needs it badly."*

---

[1]Norman Maclean, *A River Runs Through It and Other Stories* (Chicago: The University of Chicago Press, 1976), p. 81, 82.

The First Rule is Grace—
The Last Too!

In Robert Farrar Capon's book, *Between Noon and Three*, there is a section called *The Coffee Hour*. A minister has just preached a sermon on God's grace and now has asked any who would like to join together over the coffee hour and have a talk-back time with the minister. A Sheila Grinch has quietly announced that she has three daughters; she is apprehensive about our permissive society; grace sounds like you can just do anything you want to without any conscience or remorse. The minister responds.

"You're worried about permissiveness—about the way the preaching of grace seems to say it's okay to do all kinds of terrible things as long as you just walk in afterward and take the free gift of God's forgiveness.

"The first thing I think you have to say is that while you and I may be worried about seeming to give permission, Jesus apparently wasn't. He wasn't afraid of giving the prodigal son a kiss instead of a lecture, a party instead of probation; and he proved that by bringing in the elder brother at the end of the story and having him raise pretty much the same objections you do. He's angry about the party. He complains that his father is lowering standards and ignoring virtue—that music, dancing and a fatted calf are, in effect, just so many permissions to break the law. And to all that, Jesus has the father say only one thing: 'Cut that out! We're not playing good boys and bad boys any more. Your brother was dead and he's alive again. The name of the game from now on is resurrection, not bookkeeping.'

"The next thing is that when you say grace gives people permission to commit sins, you have to be very clear about what you mean. The statement needs some distinguishing. It seems to me that when I commit sin, I don't ask anyone to give me permission; I just take it. If what you're saying is that preaching grace might lead some people to do more of that, I suppose you're right.

"But that's not a *use* of the doctrine of grace, it's an *abuse*. Grace doesn't make evil good. —the law is from God, He never changes his mind about what's best for us. He doesn't back away from the law; but when push comes to shove, as it always does with us, he makes his first rule grace."[1]

". . .but the gift itself considerably outweighed the fall. If it is certain that through one man's fall so many died, it is even more certain that divine grace, coming through the one man, Jesus Christ, came to so many as an abundant free gift." Romans 5:15

The church is a moral problem when it defeats what it set out to do. It's unique mission and message is to proclaim undeserved favor, acceptance before God, and no need to work on merit badges in order to earn it. Church history and visitation to over 90 percent of the churches in this country would demonstrate that for most of her past and current history, the church has NOT been at the forefront of proclaiming this good news!

The fears are many: (1) the world doesn't work that way (that's true); (2) such a word will give permission; (3) such good news will cause people to do bad things and then ask off at the last minute. Yes, these are real fears. Yes, grace does not make sense. **And grace is the first and last unique word of the Christian community! Our task is to proclaim it and not to worry about the use or abuse that some might give grace.**

But all of these reasons are smoke screens, just like the criticisms I used to hear about the confessional booth in the Catholic church. I would hear in my youth, good protestant folk arguing that Catholics were allowed to do bad things all week because they knew they could get off on the weekend in the confessional booth. I have never known **anyone** protestant or catholic to make that kind of abusive use of the doctrine of grace.

The truth is, I don't freely proclaim grace for *your* life **because** I have not accepted grace for *my* life yet. Hence, Chesterton was right in saying: "Christianity hasn't failed; it's never really been tried."

————

[1]Robert Farrar Capon, *Between Noon and Three* (San Francisco: Harper & Row, Publishers, 1982), p. 152, 153.

The Stranger's Bargain

A teenager has just left a theatre after seeing *Star Wars*. He goes to his 1966 Chevy and it won't start. The teenager notices a man dressed in black with blonde hair standing next to a black van. They converse. Finally they exchange names, with the stranger claiming to be the devil. After rejecting and laughing off this stranger's introduction, the youth decides to play along with the joke. He tells the stranger that if he were the devil, he knows already what the devil wants. "You want my soul." The devil says he is not at all interested in his soul.

"

● ● ●if you are not interested in buying my soul, what do you want to buy? Surely not my old '66 Chevy?"

"Correct. You're a sharp young man. I do not want to buy secondhand souls or secondhand cars; my business is DREAMS. What I want to buy from you is your Dream."

"My dream?" said the young man. "Well, let's see, I had a real dilly last night. You see, I dreamt that I played the saxaphone in a Masonic marching band, and..."

"No, no, no," interrupted the Devil. "I'm not in the market for sleep-dreams or even daydreams. What I buy is THE Dream; that special vision of how you see yourself as an adult in this world. That Dream fuels your life with meaning and a rare form of excitement. It is that Dream that sets you apart from the others; in fact, from everyone else!"

"I don't understand," said the young man. "Why would you want to buy my Dream and not my soul?"

"Because, my young friend, if I were to obtain your soul I would have just a soul, but if I am able to purchase—at a fair price, mind you—your Dream, then I have changed the course of history! Your soul affects only you, but your Dream—ah, that's something different. Your Dream touches the lives of countless people and, who knows, maybe people yet to be born? The effect of your Dream is cosmic, and that's why I am interested in it."[1]

"In the days to come—it is the Lord who speaks—I will pour out my spirit on all humankind. Their sons and daughters shall prophesy, your young men shall see visions, your old men shall dream dreams." Acts 2:17 (from Joel 3:1)

I have a plaque in my office, real wood with a metal plate that reads: "I HAVE A DREAM," the now famous phrase of Martin Luther King, Jr. I bought it in 1968, the year the man who preached probably the most famous sermon of this century, died.

I remember what dreams were running through my head at the time I bought it, and put it up in my part-time-youth-minister's office. Now I look at it, 16 years later and recognize that many personal and church dreams just didn't pan out. And I realize also, what a fix I would be in right now if some of those misplaced dreams in fact did come true.

I wouldn't take the plaque down for anything though, because it holds the truth so well; the truth of what our devil friend here was saying: "kill your Dream and it is only a matter of time until you will want to die yourself."[2] Or as Martin Luther King, Jr., said in a sermon days before his own death: "the cessation of breathing is often a belated announcement of the death of the spirit that happened a long time ago."

I part company with our devil friend, who says he is not interested in night or day dreams. With night dreams, I agree. Harmless. But dreams and dreamers of the day are dangerous. For when asked "why?" they say, "Why not?" When put off by friends saying "someday," they say, "IF not now, when?"

"Having exhausted all these ways of tempting him, the devil left him, to return at the appointed time." Luke 4:13

---

[1]Edward M. Hays, *Twelve and One-Half Keys* (Easton, Kansas: Forest of Peace Books, 1981), p. 53.

[2]Ibid., p. 57.

Plenty of Time

Here's another devil story. It reads as if someone is about to tell you an old joke. It seems that the devil was having a contest in hell. Whoever could come up with the best proposal to thwart the forces of good on the earth would receive a free trip to earth to try out their plan (if you believe this story, I have some land in Nevada that glows in the dark that I would love to sell you!).

The first contestant came forward and said, "I would go and tell the people of earth that what the Holy Scriptures say is not true." The devil was unimpressed and dismissed the contestant.

The second contestant came forward and said, "I will tell them the prophets of old, the gospel writers and Jesus himself were all fake." The devil knew of the devotion to these sources of faith that people hold, and turned down the ill-thought plan.

The third contestant came forward and said, "I would like to take the trip to earth. I will infiltrate every institution and will be a good and well-known citizen. And my message to the people will be: **There is time—There is plenty of time—Don't hurry—There is plenty of time for whatever you want to do**."

Why do you think this third one won the contest?

"Here is the answer for those of you who talk like this: 'Today or tomorrow we are off to this or that town; we are going to spend a year there, trading, and make some money.' You never know what will happen tomorrow: you are no

more than a mist that is here for a little while and then disappears." James 4:13,14

Jesus called people to live radically in the present moment. He called them to live fully in the hour that was their's and to not worry about long-range plans ("eating and drinking, what to wear or what we won't have to wear"). He called people to get on with it—to get on with whatever you need to do, because life at best is precarious.

To get caught up in the myth that there is endless time to do what you need and intend to do, is the myth the junior devil winner wanted to sell. He is somewhere in the midst of our daily life right now, and thus far has proven himself a worthy winner.

How many hospital beds have rabbis and ministers been called to, to hear the recitation of this "plenty-of-time" myth. I was ushered into such a room where the president of a large corporation lay hooked up to every death-blocking machine the hospitals have. After two sudden heart attacks and now not much time left, he motioned me toward his dry mouth. He told me in whispers that he had worked 70 hours per week, saved lots of money, didn't spend much time with wife and children—was going to slow down someday, real soon. And "now it's all over" (his words, not mine).

There is time for you to do that which is most important and essential—just not as much time as you think. Whatever needs to be—get on with it! As the Hebrew sage Hillel said, "If you don't care for yourself, who will? If you care only for yourself, who are you? If not now, when?"

To Be On The Wire

The Great Wallendes were a family who, into the 1960's, fascinated millions with their high-wire act in circuses. Many, even today, remember the tragic accidents which meant death and disability to family members. After one accident where one member was killed and others seriously injured, a reporter was going to contact the father of the family, Henry Wallende. When the reporter arrived at the circus on the morning after the accident which killed and injured others of Wallende's family, he was told that Mr. Wallende was in the circus tent practicing.

The reporter had to yell him down from the wire and then asked, "What are you doing? Your family is in mourning over a death not even 24 hours ago, and you are up walking the wire. When are you going to give this up?"

The Great Wallende looked at the reporter and said: "To be on the wire is life, all else is simply waiting."[1]

"Anyone who finds his life will lose it; anyone who loses his life for my sake will find it." Matt. 10:39

Walking the high wire is not here equated with service to the Kingdom of God. The element of risk, however, is!

How many people sit on the bank, shivering, afraid to jump in—not knowing that they are colder on the bank than they would ever be in the water?

How many people do you know who have built the perfect life-savings' security in a bank book, but who have never really lived because of no risk in their existence?

How many people do you know who have found a religion, but never a relationship?

To "find life" means no specific thing. To "find life" points to a freedom that is granted to use what gifts you have for whatever significant cause you can find—and then to give those gifts!!

We hold a mistaken image about the boomerang. Ask anyone, they will tell you that a boomerang is something you fling out to the right of you and, properly thrown, will make a full circle in front of you and land at your feet. That might be the way we use the "wham-o" one we buy in the toy store, but that was not their intended use. A boomerang was made for hunting. If you hit your target, you made a catch. ONLY when you missed your target did the boomerang come back to your feet.

How many of us have, at one time or another, thought of extending ourselves in service, only to miss the target on the first try—then have said, "forget it"—and then have allowed the extended hand to pull back, quickly, until both our arms are wrapped around ourselves with the pledge that we will never get burnt like that again?

Much of ministry involves prying people's hurt and disgusted arms from around themselves—and entertaining that they, again *risk* reaching, loving, caring—risk *anything* of significance for crying out loud!—until the life promised by the Kingdom is found.

Mark Twain said, "Go out on a limb. That's where the fruit is."

When a sudden gust of wind came up while the Great Wallende was walking the high wire in Puerto Rico at the age of 72, falling awkwardly to his death, I was silent with quiet shock. But, I did not shed a tear. Instead I remembered the words of a man who inspired me and many others—the one who said, "To be on the wire is life; everything else is simply waiting."

---

[1]Bruce Larson, *Risky Christianity* (Waco: Word, Inc., 1981), p. 89.

Five Lanterns At Sundown

Perhaps the story of the wise and foolish virgins at the wedding is one of the earliest stories deposited in my mind. I can still see my first grade teachers flannel board in church school. The point was clear—five were wise to bring enough oil for the night; five were foolish and didn't bring enough. It's important to be prepared!! (The Scouts like this idea too.)

Like all Biblical stories given in first grade—you just learn the story. That's all. Implications and lessons are not ready to be discovered until much later. On the other hand, even much later, I'm not sure that many of us, inside and outside the church, get beyond a first grade understanding with such passages.

One author summed up this passage by saying: "You see, I still get all riled up when I think about it. I kind of lose control. In my more objective moments, I recognize that what happened that night made no difference whatsoever. The essential things—the decisive things—had happened before sunset, before that day even. *The events of that night were the logical conclusion to the deep decisions the (two groups of five) had made long ago.*"[1]

"So stay awake, because you do not know the day when your master is coming." Matt. 24:42

Talk of the end of the world is in. Biblical or nuclear end—people are buying books that talk about it.

As early as Paul, the word "watch" confused people. He had to deal with people becoming irresponsible with family, job and paying their charge accounts on time because people literally were standing on the mountain looking for the return, bodily, of Jesus. Kress said it all, talk of the end of the world, the last days "are children's clothes that a religion has to shuck before it can become adult. They are children's dreams that the powerless must invent to console themselves. But in modern society the citizens have the power, and we can work for a better world here, not just 'pie-in-the-sky-when-you-die.' "[2]

A mature Christian is one who will take the words "watch" and "beware" as overarching pointers for life, not words which point to a day and a week. As one woman said, "Tuesday, January 17. The Kingdom of God is not in the clouds. It's here, in the United Nations, in Common Cause, and in the Sierra Club, AND I'M WORKING FOR IT![3] What's more—how could anyone have the audacity to worry about an end-time initiated by God at a time when the human family, in all the freedom granted by God, has the power in not too many buttons to end life on this planet forever?

"Therefore, watch. . ." not the clouds, but your next move. For in each movement of your life for peace, the Kingdom comes.

---

[1]Alfred C. Kress, *Five Lanterns At Sundown* (Grand Rapids: William B. Eerdmans Publish Company, 1978), p. 4.
[2]Ibid., p. 17.
[3]Ibid., p. 17.

Arms Linked
On A Mourner's Bench

This section is a quote from J. H. Bowden, as he summarizes and gives an overview to Peter DeVries' book, *The Blood of the Lamb.* The main character is a Mr. Wanderhope whose daughter, Carol, is dying of leukemia. Her final moment approaches—

"The crisis hurries on: Carol is stigmatized on hands and breast by needles and probes. Her hair falls out; she has gone from fairy to troll. Then comes remission, then an infection that hits hardest those whose blood can't handle it. Wanderhope has come to bring a cake to Carol because it's her birthday, but left it in St. Catherine's, where he'd gone to pray. Seeing Carol, he 'knew it was time to say good-by.' When the nurse steps outside he prays: 'The Lord bless thee, and keep thee: The Lord make his face shine upon thee, and be gracious unto thee: The Lord lift up his countenance upon thee, and give thee peace.' At three in the afternoon—at the same time as did Jesus—she dies.

"Wanderhope wishes taking leave of her were like Hemingway's 'saying good-by to a statue,' but she looks instead 'like some mangled flower, or like a bird that had been pelted to death in a storm.' He gets drunk at a nearby bar, then remembers the cake. In the by now carefully set up scene he balances it for a moment, then hurls the cake onto the face of the corpse: Christ has pied him, now he Christ. 'Then through scalded eyes I seemed to see the hands free themselves of the nails and move slowly toward the soiled face. Very slowly, very deliberately, with infinite patience, the icing was wiped from the eyes and flung away.' And he hears a voice saying,

'Suffer the little children to come unto me. . .for of such is the kingdom of heaven.'

"His attempt to recover at his daughter's grave the piety lost at his brother's is not successful; when he plays a tape to hear her recorded pieces he gets as well a message from Carol in which she quotes with approbation his credo sent to his college magazine: Reason, Courage, and Grace have sustained her, she says, and she knows about her disease. Wanderhope flings away his crucifix, flings it into the trees of the woods where they had walked. The world is hateful, and progress only enlarges our stay in it. Grace is ours, but to give rather than receive; and compassion is gained as one realizes 'how long is the mourner's bench upon which we sit, arms linked in undeluded friendship, all of us, brief links, ourselves, in the eternal pity.' "

"And he saved us from dying, as he will save us again; yes, that is our firm hope in him, that in the future he will save us again." II Corinthians 1:10

The most often quoted sermon of Dr. William Sloane Coffin, Jr., is the sermon he preached less than two weeks after the death of his son Alex. In San Antonio, Texas he told me, "if the story I told helps others, then it helps me." Here is what he said in his sermon entitled *Alex's Death...*

"As almost all of you know, a week ago last Monday night, driving in a terrible storm, my son Alexander—who to his friends was a real day-brightener, and to his family 'fair as a star when only one is shining in the sky'—my twenty-four-year-old Alexander, who enjoyed beating his old man at every game and in every race, beat his father to the grave....

"When a person dies, there are many things that can be said, and there is at least one thing that should never be said. The night after Alex died I was sitting in the living room of my sister's house outside of Boston, when the front door opened and in came a nice-looking middle-aged woman, carrying about eighteen quiches. When she saw me she shook her head, then headed for the kitchen, saying sadly over her shoulder, 'I just don't understand the will of God.' Instantly I was up and in hot pursuit, swarming all over her. 'I'll say you don't lady!' I said. (I knew the anger would do me good, and the instruction to her was long overdue.) I continued, 'Do you think it was the will of God that Alex never fixed that lousy windshield wiper of his, that he was probably driving too fast in such a storm, that he probably had had a couple of frosties too many? Do you think it is God's will that there are no streetlights along that stretch of road, and no guard rail separating the road and Boston Harbor?'

"For some reason, nothing so infuriates me as the incapacity of seemingly intelligent people to get it through their heads that God doesn't go around this world with his finger on triggers, his fist around knives, his hands on steering wheels. God is dead-set against all unnatural deaths. And Christ spent an inordinate amount of time delivering people from paralysis, insanity, leprosy, and muteness. Which is not to say that there are no nature-caused deaths, deaths that are untimely and slow and pain-ridden, which for that reason raise unanswerable questions. . .But violent deaths, such as the one Alex died—to understand those is a piece of cake. As his younger brother put it simply, standing at the head of the casket at the Boston funeral, 'You blew it, buddy. You blew it.' The one thing that should never be said when someone dies is, 'It is the will of God.' Never do we know enough to say that. My own consolation lies in knowing that it was **not** the will of God that Alex died; **that when the waves closed over the sinking car, God's heart was the first of all our hearts to break.**"

Amen.

Hollow Halos

My dearest Shauna:

Perhaps it seems strange to you that I, your minister, would be writing you personally after your performance in last Sunday night's Christmas pageant. It seems that there was no one else to turn to who could truly understand me, and so I chose you. Even though just five years of age, I know we can relate because of our like experiences.

I want you to know that if any children should have been chosen to be angels in the Christmas pageant, you and Ashley would be my best choices. You two are angels, believe me.

Then I want you to know the moment that I knew I would be writing and seeking you out. I guess it was in the second musical number (wasn't it?) that you had a problem that has haunted me all my life. Shauna, when your halo was slipping badly, I knew you and I were finally going to be friends for life. When that coat-hanger-sprayed-with-gold started to buckle, bend and slip, my whole life passed in front of me.

Suddenly every teacher clear through high school passed in front of my face. I remembered the halo I tried to wear that made me look like a good student while not doing any homework, or bluffing my way through it all. I remember when that halo slipped, bent and buckled badly and I was revealed for what I really was.

Then I remembered the halo bought in my late teen years that was marked "minister." I look back now and realize how "perfect" in the worst sense of the word that I wanted to be. Then suddenly all my halos got bent. I ran in to some real fine teachers who stopped short my charade and said: "you will get this or you are out!" And I needed that.

Then my professional halo was next to go. I knew inside that I was a hotshot that was going to make churches, any churches, GROW and be bulging at the seams just because I was there. And, Shauna, you can't believe how bent that halo got. I found that I just couldn't make those church assignments grow and worse yet, I was angry about it and wouldn't admit it.

Then my private halo slipped. Do you know what it means to have someone say that they can't remember anyone getting a divorce in the family as far back as they can remember? Shauna, by that time my halos were so badly bent. . .I can't hardly talk about it.

What I'm saying is that when your halo slipped, I remembered all mine—the many halos I bought which slipped badly. And now, thank God, my halos have been abandoned forever and life is better. I discovered the hard way that God doesn't want us buying halos, but that He wants us to buy into happiness that is found only when we finally accept our frail selves just half as much as he has already accepted us.

And now, Shauna, you know what I want for Christmas? At 41 years of age I want the child part of me to be set loose on a stage—just like you were—and on that stage I want all my halos to freely slip—and I want to hear the laughter that comes when the halos finally hit the floor—and I want to know that they do not laugh *at me*, but *with me*. On that stage of falling halos will be this truth: our best shots and all our best efforts often come up short—and the laughter that is heard is finally *ours* when we realize that God didn't want us perfect—but only at peace. A peace that comes when we finally accept ourselves as we are and give only what we have. For that is enough. And in that moment we will know love in a new key.

Halo to you, Dear Shauna. And Merry Christmas. Your bent-halo friend, Dick.

*"...but however great the number of sins com-
mitted, grace was even greater. Romans 5:20*

All Is the Same; All Is New

It was 6:00 A.M. Our church's 24-hour prayer vigil was in progress. There is an unofficial rule that the minister of the congregation fills in on those hours no one else wants. So there I was, alone, liking the moment to the degree that I could stay awake.

An older book was there for my meditational use. Its title is *Like the Great Mountains*, by Jack Finegan, a good teacher from my denomination who taught many years at Pacific School of Religion. The book was dedicated to the "Members and friends of the First

Christian Church, Concord, California, who have listened with inspiring attention and encouraging interest to some of these messages." The date was October 26, 1949.

His last chapter was titled, "The Challenge to Modern Youth."[1] The agenda that Finegan set for the youth of 1949 was:

1. **To work for international cooperation.** He notes that as a nation we are not inclined toward brotherhood but are strictly loners. "We plead that America should attempt neither to isolate itself nor to dominate the world but to cooperate with the rest of the world. Only by such cooperation in fearless friendliness with all nations, both large and small, can lasting peace be achieved."

2. **To strive for racial equality.** Finegan called this the most pressing need at home. "This is a problem which has long been left unsolved and which threatens to break forth in violence."

3. **To share economic opportunity more widely.** He deplored the conditions of slums which breeds disease, crime and dependency.

"The freedom of the individual Christian person must be matched by their sense of social responsibility."

4. **To uphold social idealism.** Here he lifts up the dangers of alcoholism, crime and materialism.

5. **To accomplish Christian unity.** He cites the confusion of religious sects and denominations in the United States. "A weak, divided, and contentious church can never lead America toward great Christian goals. We need to work for the increasing unity of all Christian people. . . ."

I read all this—in a small chapel—at 6:00 A.M.—30 years after these lofty ideals were lifted—and I cried!

"*. . .our hope (is) THAT HE WILL DELIVER US AGAIN.*" II Corinthians 1:10

So here we have Dr. Jack Finegan, writing and dedicating his cutting-edge sermons of his day to the First Christian Church of Concord in 1949. Here I sit, assembling meditations that I will dedicate the same way.

AND my mind wanders, cynically, as I view the old checklist and the day in which we live. International cooperation is at a dangerously low ebb, what with all those bombs we have pointed at each other. The racial violence predicted did come. Response was made. Some things got better. Today we live with an outright vindictive attitude toward those in need, most especially minority groups. Promises of ghetto reforms have flourished with few changes. To the dangers of alcohol and materialism, we add drug usage, not perceived by anyone as a serious threat in 1949. Ecumenical talk is only that, and for the time being falls on deaf ears.

There is lots of room for cynicism. Much talk about the new, while all seems to be the same!

And where then is our hope? Hope that doesn't get specific is no hope at all. So where is our hope? At the same place it has always been. Our hope is not so much in our changing circumstances in the world, but in being able to change *our angle of vision*. That is the new thing we can create; that is the new moment we can make. By being able to see specifically, rather than generally, we can see the tree that grows in Brooklyn as well as the singing of the caged bird and all the other things that are right and beautiful in a world that doesn't know how to solve in any age the BIG problems.

In Ingmar Bergman's *Fanny and Alexander,* we follow the life, love and mysteries of a family of actors and actresses. Toward the close of the film is a family reunion, and a toast is given by the head of the Ekdahl family:

"...we Ekdahls have not come into the world to see through it, never think that. We are not equipped for such excursions. We might just as well ignore the big things. We must live in the little, the little world. We shall be content with that and cultivate it and make the best of it....We must be able to grasp the world and reality, so that we can complain of its monotony with a clear conscience. Dear, splendid actors and actresses, we need you all the same. It is you who are to give us our supernatural shudders and still more our mundane amusements. . . .Therefore it is necessary, and not in the least shameful, to take pleasure in the little world, good food, gentle smiles, fruit-trees in bloom, waltzes."[2]

We are a part of this family, and then again, not. We WILL NOT ignore the big things, but will bring them daily into focus because since ancient times, the needs of the poor, neglected, starving and lost in life always belong to our care as the highest expression of what it means to be a part of the Kingdom. While voicing the big concerns, we will dare live in the little world with our theology of small victories and our alertness to the tiny ways our will can coincide with God's.

---

[1]Jack Finegan, *Like the Great Mountains* (St. Louis: Bethany Press, 1949), p. 152-159.

[2]Ingmar Bergman, *Fanny and Alexander* (New York: Pantheon Books, 1982), p. 207, 208.

ABOUT THE AUTHOR

Richard A. Wing is the Senior Minister of the University Christian Church, San Diego, California. He is a graduate of Northwest Christian College, Eugene, Oregon ('66) and the School of Theology at Claremont ('70). This is his first book, inspired by the Celebration of the 100th Anniversary of the congregation he served in Concord, California.

Additional copies of this book may be purchased for $9.95 per copy plus $1.50 for postage and handling (total of $11.45). California residents send $12.10 (includes tax, postage and handling). Send to:

ARTHUR PUBLISHING
P. O. Box 33213
San Diego, California 92103-0400